How do Animals Talk?

Susan Mayes

Designed by Claire Littlejohn, Brian Robertson and Mary Forster
Illustrated by Angela Hargreaves, Philip Hood and Colin King
Consultant: Joyce Pope
Cover design by Russell Punter
Cover illustration by Christyan Fox
With thanks to Sarah Cronin

KT-170-431

CONTENTS

Ways of talking

People talk to each other for all kinds of reasons. They talk using words, but they also say things in other ways. Different movements, sounds and faces all help you say what you mean.

This face shows sadness.

A "shhh" sound helps you say "be quiet".

You may greet your best friends by stretching out your arms out to them.

Watching your pets

Animals say things to each other all the time. They don't use words, but they do "talk" in other ways, just as we do. Try watching your pets to see what they do.

You may see your dog bow to another dog like this. He is saying "play with me". He may do this to you too.

If your dog pokes another dog in the side with his nose, he is saying "stand still".

Life in the wild

In the wild, animals have to "talk" to each other so that they can survive and bring up their families. For example, this is important for the cat's wild relative, the lion.

A lioness's special scent tells males when she is ready to mate.

Lioness

The parents and their babies must understand each other so the family can stay safely together.

Lionesses teach their cubs to hunt and to protect themselves.

Lion

Cubs

Lionesses

Lions guard their own bit of land, telling others to keep away.

When lions hunt together they must understand each other's movements, so they can catch food more easily.

If you have pet cats you will often see them rubbing noses like this in a friendly greeting.

Animals "talk" to each other with many movements, sounds and smells. Some have special colours and patterns.

These all make clear messages which are full of important information for family, friends and even enemies.

Saying "keep out"

The place where an animal finds food, water and a mate is very important. The animal guards part of it, to keep away others of its own kind.

The area the animal guards is called its territory. Territory owners must make clear warnings which tell others "keep out, I live here".

Making a noise

Many animals make sounds to warn others "this is my territory". Noises are a good warning because they travel a long way.

Birds such as gulls make a simple call which says "this is mine". Other birds, such as thrushes, sing more complicated songs.

Each kind of bird has a different song. Usually, the male sings it. He learns it by listening to the adult males when he is young.

When the bird is ready to guard terrritory of his own, he adds new bits to his song. This makes a stronger "keep out" signal.

A bird's song is usually meant for birds of his own kind. This thrush is singing to warn other thrushes nearby.

This thrush recognizes his neighbour's song and will keep out of his territory.

Rat-a-tat-tat

A male woodpecker marks his territory with a loud rat-a-tat-tat. He makes the sound by drumming his beak on a hollow branch or tree.

The lion's roar

Lions live in groups called prides. A pride's territory can be up to twenty kilometres across.

An adult male warns other males away with an almighty roar. It can be heard eight kilometres away.

The woodpecker in this picture makes about 25 drums a second. When he is feeding he only makes a short tap-tap.

Noises underwater

The male haddock guards his underwater territory by making noises. He moves special muscles so they drum against a part called his swim bladder.

If a haddock is very angry with another male, the drumming becomes so quick it sounds like a loud hum.

Internet links Go to **www.usborne-quicklinks.com** for links to websites where you can listen to lots of animal sounds and find out how animals protect their territory.

More warnings

Different animals have different ways of saying "keep out of my territory". Bright colours, claw marks and strong smells are all warnings to strangers.

Some animals make themselves look bigger than they really are.

You may have seen a cat's hair stand on end if a strange cat comes into the garden. This is called a display.

Warning colour

When a male stickleback fish is ready to build his nest and look for a mate, his tummy turns bright red.

If he sees the red tummy of another male in his territory he gets very angry and chases the fish away.

A male elephant seal opens his mouth in an enormous gape to frighten other males away from his territory.

The Australian frilled lizard raises its bright neck flap and opens its mouth wide if an enemy comes too close.

Internet link Go to **www.usborne-quicklinks.com** for a link to a website where you can find out more about how animals protect themselves.

Smelly messages

Many animals have a very good sense of smell and they mark their territories with smelly messages.

An otter marks its exit from the water by leaving droppings on a stone.

The scent of a dropping can last for many weeks.

Dogs mark places where they live and walk by urinating (weeing). First, they sniff to smell who else has been there.

"I was here"

Bears mark their territory by scratching at trees. The claw marks warn other bears "I was here".

Stink fights

Male ring-tailed lemurs have stink fights to win territory. Their smelly scent is made under the skin of their arms.

Each lemur pulls his tail between his arms, then he waves it about. The one with the strongest scent usually wins.

Finding a mate

Most kinds of animals look for a mate each year, so they can have babies.

The meeting place

Each year Uganda kobs meet at a place called a lek. The males gather there to fight for small bits of territory. A female visits a male's territory when she is ready to find a mate.

This male is displaying to a female who has come into his territory. He is showing off by dancing near her, to see if she will be his partner.

Usually, a male makes signals to a female, inviting her to be his partner.

These male kobs are fighting for territory. The weaker animal will give in.

Beautiful birds

Male birds are usually more colourful than female birds. They use their brightly coloured feathers to make beautiful displays to the female birds.

A male blue bird of paradise hangs upside down and fans out his blue and green feathers.

Calling out

Many male animals tell females where they are by calling out to them. Male frogs call to the females by making loud croaking noises.

This frog's croak sounds loud because it echoes inside his puffed-out pouch.

A male bush cricket calls to a female by rubbing his wings together.

Smelling the air

Some animals, like this male gypsy moth, can smell a mate from far away. The moth's big antennae help him smell a female moth's special scent.

A male golden pheasant circles his mate. He opens a feathery fan on the side of his head which is closest to her.

A peacock stands in front of the female, the peahen, and displays to her by shaking his enormous curved feathers.

Internet link Go to **www.usborne-quicklinks.com** for a link to a website where you can listen to bird calls and discover some of the different ways birds attract mates.

Family talk

Animal parents and their babies must talk to each other for many reasons. They need to know how to recognize each other, so the family can stay safely together. They must also understand each other when they feed.

A voice from the egg

Some baby animals talk with their mother even before they are born.

Chicks make cheeping noises while they are still in the shell and the hen answers.

A female Nile crocodile buries her eggs in the sand. When the babies are ready to hatch they make a peeping call. The mother hears the noise and uncovers the eggs, so the babies can get out.

"Are you my mother?"

Many baby animals learn to recognize their parents almost as soon as they are born. This is called imprinting.

When birds hatch, their parents are usually the first things they see. These ducklings are following their mother.

Hungry chicks

Many kinds of chicks have brightly coloured throats. This colour is a signal to the parents. When they see it they feed their hungry babies.

In some birds, the parents have colourful signalling marks.

An adult gull has a bright spot on the bottom part of its beak. When a chick sees the colour it taps the spot. This makes the parent bring up food which it has been storing inside its body.

Important smells

Some animals recognize each other by smell. A female sheep learns the smell and taste of her lambs. She will not look after another mother's lamb.

This sheep can recognize the voice of her lamb among the bleating of all the other lambs.

Sometimes, the first thing a baby animal sees is not its real parent, but another animal.

These baby geese have never seen their real mother. They have imprinted on a dog and they follow it everywhere.

Living together

Many animals spend their lives together, in a group. Here are some of the ways they say things to each other with their bodies and faces.

Chimpanzee language

Chimpanzees often talk using different movements, just as we do.

Chimps sometimes show they are friendly by kissing when they meet.

A chimp greets a more important member of the group by holding out its hand. The other one shows it is friendly by touching the hand.

Chimps calm each other by hugging and touching.

Making faces

Chimps make many different faces to say how they feel. They also add to their messages with different calls.

This chimp's smile shows that it is happy. Your smile says the same thing.

This chimp seems to be laughing, but it is not happy at all. It is frightened.

This hard stare means that the chimp is angry and may attack.

Internet link Go to **www.usborne-quicklinks.com** *for a link to a website where you can listen to wolves howl.*

An angry gorilla

An adult male gorilla makes a frightening and noisy warning display if he feels threatened.

As part of the display the gorilla beats his chest. The loud booming sound can be heard far away.

Showing who is boss

In many groups each animal has a place in order of importance. This is called the pecking order. Wolves in a pack signal with their faces and tails to show their position.

This is the pack leader. His ears stand up and point forward. He holds his tail higher than the others.

When the pack leader is near, this less important wolf flattens his ears and drops his tail between his legs.

These wolves are fighting to be the pack leader. The loser rolls on to his back, showing his throat to the winner.

Looking for food

Some kinds of animals hunt and feed in groups. It is easier to find food when there are lots of pairs of eyes keeping a look-out.

It is also easier to spy danger. Here are some of the ways different animals say things to each other when they are looking for food.

African hunting dogs

Before a hunt, African hunting dogs get ready by licking and nudging each other. They soon get excited and set off together.

On the hunt, the dogs' strong scent helps them keep in contact. Their white-tipped tails help them to see each other.

Afterwards, the hunters will go back to their den to feed the puppies and dogs who stayed behind.

The hungry dogs ask for food by licking the hunters' lips. Then the hunters bring up bits of meat which they ate at the kill.

Internet link Go to www.usborne-quicklinks.com for a link to a website with photographs and information about the things ants like to eat.

Smelly trails

A family of ants is called a colony. The worker ants search for food. They leave scent trails as they go. When a worker ant finds plenty of food it takes some back to the nest.

Some more workers leave the nest and find the food by following the trail. They smell the scent with their antennae.

Worker ants are females. This one is tapping the ground with her antennae so she can smell where to go.

Feeding the flock

Different kinds of small songbirds sometimes gather in a flock to hunt for berries and seeds. They call to each other to say where there is food or to warn enemies.

The birds make about 25 different sounds, each with a special meaning.

"Come and help"

Sometimes an ant finds a bit of food which is too big for it to carry, so it tells the others to "come and help". It does this by hitting them with its antennae and front legs.

Different kinds of ants eat different food. Some eat plants and some eat other creatures. These black ants eat both.

Busy bees

There can be as many as fifty thousand bees in a honeybee colony. Colonies are made up of three kinds of bees.

The worker bees are females. They collect food, do the cleaning and feed the queen. They do not lay eggs.

The drone bees are males. They mate with a few special females who then become queens of new colonies.

The queen is the biggest and most important bee. Each hive has one queen. She lays eggs and is the mother of all the bees.

The queen's scent

Bees crowd around the queen. They try to touch her and lick her.

The queen bee has a strong scent which has a powerful effect on the rest of the colony. As long as the queen is there the bees work calmly.

Strangers beware

Every bee colony has its own scent. Sometimes, a stranger from another colony tries to get into the hive, but the bees recognize its different scent and push it out.

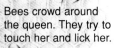

The intruder curls up. This tells the other bees "I give in".

Internet link Go to www.usborne-quicklinks.com *for a link to a website where you can watch video clips of bees waggle dancing.*

"Food is this way"

Honeybees visit flowers to collect pollen and sweet food called nectar. When a worker bee finds plenty of food, she tells the others where to find it by doing a special dance.

The waggle dance

If a bee finds food far away from the hive she dances in the shape of a squashed figure 8. In the straight part she waggles her body very quickly.

This waggling part of the dance is called the waggle run.

The speed of the dance and the direction of the waggle run tell the bees how far away the food is. They also tell the bees which way to fly.

The round dance

If the food is nearby the dancer moves in a circle, going one way then the other way.

The bees touch her and copy her. They can smell the pollen on her fur, so they know which kind of flower to look for.

When the bees find the flowers they collect food. They then return to the hive and do the dance themselves.

Staying safe

Animals mostly say just things to their own kind, but if they are in danger, they say things to other creatures too. They even say things to their enemies.

Patterned warnings

Poisonous animals often have bright patterns which tell enemies "don't eat me, I'm dangerous". Attackers get a nasty shock if they ignore the warning. They soon learn to keep away.

A wasp can give a nasty sting. Its yellow and black stripes are a bright "danger" warning.

This coral snake is very poisonous. Its red, yellow and black bands are a clear warning to other animals.

If this sort of boxfish is frightened it gives off a poisonous slime. Its colourful pattern tells enemies that it is dangerous to come near.

A sudden surprise

Some animals escape from an attacker by surprising it. This moth looks the same colour as the tree it is resting on, but its bright hind wings are hidden.

If the moth is disturbed, it flies and startles the attacker with a flash of colour. Then it settles again. The attacker thinks the moth has gone.

"I'm watching you"

Some animals are born with a clever disguise. They have markings which look like big eyes, which can frighten or confuse an enemy.

If the eyed hawk-moth is disturbed it moves its front wings to show two big spots underneath. They look like the eyes of a big animal.

The elephant hawk-moth caterpillar has large eye markings. These make the front of its body look like a snake's head.

Many kinds of butterfly fish have a dark spot near the tail. This confuses enemies as they think they are looking at the head.

An early warning

When some birds sense danger they make a loud, frightened call. Other kinds of birds understand there is something wrong and join in.

If you hear lots of excited bird-calls in a garden, it may mean there is a cat about.

Internet link Go to **www.usborne-quicklinks.com** for a link to a website where you can find out about deadly but colourful sea slugs.

Talking underwater

Whales, dolphins and many kinds of fish use sounds, movements and even smells to say things in their underwater world. Sound is a strong signal as it travels well in water.

Dolphin language

Dolphins live in groups called schools. They say things with lots of noises, including squawks, whistles, groans, burps and clicks.

Hawaiian spinner dolphins are most noisy in the evenings, when they are about to go hunting.

When they are ready to leave, they all join in a special chorus of noises. They also leap and slap the water with their bodies. This helps to show where everyone is before they go.

Whales

Whales call to each other with loud sounds which other whales can hear from far away. They make high trumpeting noises and low grunting sounds.

Scientists think the noises may help the whales keep in touch with each other when they are far apart.

Mystery songs

Humpback whales make sounds which they repeat in long, complicated patterns. Scientists call these "songs", but nobody knows what the songs mean.

A humpback whale usually sings when it is looking for a mate. A song can last for over 30 minutes.

Internet link Go to **www.usborne-quicklinks.com** for a link to a website where you can listen to the sounds that whales make.

Noisy fish

Many fish make sounds by rubbing their teeth, bones or fin spines together. Some even make sounds by moving muscles in their bodies.

This is called a grunt fish. It makes a grunting noise by grinding teeth which grow in its throat.

Scientists think these sounds help the fish say things to the rest of its group.

Alarm signal

If a minnow is hurt by an attacker, its body sends out a special liquid from the wound.

This signal says "danger" and the other minnows keep away.

Dancing fish

This colourful male guppy fish is showing the female that he wants to be her mate.

He does this by dancing up to her and fanning out his beautiful fins.

The whale may sing its song over and over again for many hours, without a rest.

Whales change their songs and add new bits. They can even remember a song from one year to the next.

Dogs and people

Internet link *Go to www.usborne-quicklinks.com for a link to a website where you can watch a slide show about dogs and how they help humans.*

For hundreds of years people have trained dogs, using a language of signals and commands. Dogs are very sensitive. They can tell a lot from small changes in their owner's voice. This helps to make them easy to train.

Trained to help

Wolves and wild dogs follow their pack leader and do what it tells them. Animals who live or work with people obey a human leader instead.

Dogs can be trained to herd sheep. The farmer whistles signals which tell the dogs what to do.

Some dogs are trained to guide blind people. They obey their owners, but if there is danger, the dog gives the orders. If there is something in the way, the dog stops its owner from moving.

Police dog handlers are taught to train their own dogs. The handler and the dog must learn to trust and understand each other.

Sheepdogs are good at their job because their wild relatives herded their prey when they hunted.

This dog is being trained to track down criminals.

Internet links

For links to more websites about animals, go to the Usborne Quicklinks Website at **www.usborne-quicklinks.com** and click on the number of the website you want to visit.

Website 1 – Find out lots about animals in an online A to Z guide, with pictures to print out.

Website 2 – Take a sound safari and listen to different animals found around the world.

Website 3 – Play a penguin game and find out how penguins communicate.

Website 4 – Watch video clips, read fascinating facts and solve interactive quizzes about the ways different animals communicate.

Website 5 – See if you can learn how to interact with a troop of chimps - your survival depends on it!

Website 6 – Find out how to become a dog trainer or look at other jobs working with animals.

Website 7 – Meet Koko, a gorilla who has been communicating with humans for more than twenty-five years, then try an interactive game and see if you can learn some gorilla sign language.

Website 8 – The environment where an animal lives is known as its habitat and here you can choose a habitat and find out about the animals that live there or play interactive games to discover even more about animals.

Index